B. P. Pratten

The Scottish National Portrait Gallery

The building and its contents. Also a report of the opening ceremony.

B. P. Pratten

The Scottish National Portrait Gallery
The building and its contents. Also a report of the opening ceremony.

ISBN/EAN: 9783337240257

Printed in Europe, USA, Canada, Australia, Japan

Cover: Foto ©Thomas Meinert / pixelio.de

More available books at **www.hansebooks.com**

THE SCOTTISH NATIONAL PORTRAIT GALLERY

THE SCOTTISH NATIONAL PORTRAIT GALLERY

The Building and its Contents
Also a Report of the
Opening Ceremony

Compiled by the Curator

EDINBURGH

1891

Edinburgh
George Waterston & Sons
Printers

LIST OF ILLUSTRATIONS.

The arms on title-page show the undifferenced royal shield of Scotland,
as stamped on binding of a copy of 'Ambrosio Augustino &c.,
Collectanea'. . . . Philoth Iræneo autore; Basilex 1542,
from the library of James Stuart, prior of St Andrews,
afterwards Earl of Murray. The imprint on final
page is the figure of Sir David Lindsay of
the Mount, Lyon King of Arms,
from the title-page of his
'Ane Dialog betuix
E x p e r i e n c e,
&c.' Paris,
1558

THE SCOTTISH NATIONAL PORTRAIT GALLERY.

COTLAND cherishes the memory of her distinguished sons ; and, since art first took firm root in the country, she has been fortunate in having had a succession of capable painters well able to record their aspect in the flesh. Jamesone of Aberdeen, the first quite definite and authentic figure in Scottish art, was almost exclusively a portrait-painter. Raeburn was a portrait-painter, and that only ; and it was in portraiture that Watson Gordon won his fame. Even the greatest of the Scottish figure-painters, though their life-work has been the portrayal of the human drama, the rendering of all the vivid changeful play of men in action one with another, have not disdained the occasional practice of the more restricted branch of art ; and men like Wilkie and Duncan in the past, like Orchardson in our own time, have produced portraits so vigorous or so delicate as to be, in themselves alone, the sufficient foundation of a great artistic reputation.

And that—recently at least—Scotland has done her part in preserving and making visible the portraits of her great men, is sufficiently apparent from the account given by the Lord Justice-General (in his speech quoted in the Appendix) of the various Portrait Loan Exhibitions which, from time to time, have been held in our country. Each of these did good work in interesting the public in the subject of National Portraiture, and in

preparing the way for the more important and decisive step of
the foundation of the Scottish National Portrait Gallery, which,
begun in temporary premises in 1885, was formally opened to the
public in the permanent Gallery, Queen Street, Edinburgh, in
July 1889.

The Official Catalogue of the Gallery gives a concise description of each item in the collection, biographical notes of the
persons represented, and full information as to the sources from
which the various works have been obtained. The aim of the
present Pamphlet is somewhat slighter and more general. It
is intended here to furnish a brief account of the Galleries themselves, and of the chief portraits which they contain, regard-
ing the latter chiefly from their national and historical side, as
illustrating the achievements of Scotsmen in the various departments of human endeavour. Exterior and interior views of the
building are also given, along with reproductions of a selection
of the more notable portraits ; and an account of the ceremony
on the occasion of the opening of the Gallery is subjoined in an
Appendix.

The edifice has been designed by Dr R. Rowand Anderson,
Architect to the Honourable the Board of Trustees for Manufactures, in the Gothic style of the thirteenth century, and its
design was awarded a gold medal at the Munich Annual Exhibition of 1890. It is built of red Corsehill stone of a warm and
mellow tone. The entire length of the structure measures 264
feet, its breadth 71 feet. In the North Front, of which views,
taken from the north-east and north-west, are given in our
Frontispiece and Illustration No. I., the ground floor shows a
series of wide arched windows, severe in outline, and, structur-
ally, excellently adapted for sustaining the superposed weight of
masonry. Above each of these appears a pair of smaller, pointed
windows, which light the first-floor Galleries, divided in their

centres by shafts of grey granite supporting the tracery that fills their upper portion. Each of the pairs in which these first-floor windows are arranged is separated from the rest by a canopied niche, designed for the reception of the statue of an eminent Scotsman ; and, between the tops of these windows and the stone balustrade—strengthened and ornamented at intervals by floriated piers—surmounting the whole, the walls of the highest roof-lighted storey are carried round the building as a space of blank wall, which gives great dignity to the façade. Besides the enrichments of the windows and of the porch, the building is adorned by four angle turrets, which are corbelled out, from square buttresses, into an octagonal form, at the first-floor level, and are surmounted by decorated spires of stone. The east lateral wall of the building is also treated with considerable richness and variety. The western side is somewhat plainer ; while the southern side, facing towards St Andrew Street Lane, is marked by extreme simplicity, and owes its effect entirely to its well-calculated proportions and restrained severity of line.

The chief entrance to the Galleries forms a prominent central feature of the northern front of the building. The porch, flanked on either side by buttresses recessed with niches intended for statues, is carried up nearly the entire height of the edifice, and terminates in a gable, surmounting a cusped arch, the spandrels within and beneath which are at present left in rough masonry, but are eventually to be carved with sculpture in relief as part of the general scheme of exterior decoration.

Passing through the Vestibule, we have access by arched openings into a lofty Central Hall, extending through the ground and first floor storeys of the building, and surrounded by an arcading, in two heights, of solid circular pillars and yet more massive corner piers. These support sharply-curved, well-proportioned pointed arches, the lower tier being surmounted

by those of the first-floor ambulatory. Here already in this Hall, the portraiture of the Gallery begins, for beside each of the piers a large marble bust has been placed, and a full-length statue of **Burns** by Flaxman occupies the south-east corner, beneath the arcading.

The door in the centre of the eastern wall of the Hall admits to that portion of the building devoted to the preservation and exhibition of the National Museum of Antiquities, and including its Library and Offices.

Leaving the Hall, and turning to our right, the west and north doors admit to two large Galleries on the ground floor. The former of these and a smaller apartment in the west wing have at present been let on a short lease to the Royal Scottish Geographical Society ; and the latter forms a Lecture Hall, available for use by the Geographical Society, and for such other bodies who may rent it from the Board of Manufactures.

Access to the first-floor Galleries is obtained by a broad flight of stairs, where the wide segmental curves of the arches overhead oppose with excellent effect the sharper forms of the lancet-shaped lights of the windows. The walls are lined with smooth red brick ; and the brackets which sustain busts at the landings have grey granite columns and richly-sculptured capitals, repeating the scheme of the external decoration of the building.

On the first floor are two large Galleries (Illustration No. II.), similar to those on the ground floor to which we have already referred, but separated only by a series of wide and open arches : and here the main portion of the collection of Scottish National Portraits is at present hung, the wall-space being supplemented by a series of simply-designed wooden screens.

From these Galleries we pass to the Ambulatory (Illustration No. III.), overlooking the Central Hall, which is furnished with a

TCH

gracefully-designed railing of wrought-iron, the walls being decorated with busts arranged on stone brackets, and the south-east and south-west corners occupied by colossal statues. The doors to the north give admission to a series of three smaller apartments, a Board Room and a couple of Business Rooms.

Ascending another flight of stairs, we gain the top storey, and enter the most spacious of all the Galleries, the large Hall, carried above the central Entrance Hall, and stretching the entire breadth of the building (Illustration No. IV.) It is lighted from the top by a cupola, towards which the cove of the ceiling curves gracefully, and is recessed on its northern side by an arcading of arches. The southern wall of this Gallery is at present devoted to the Scottish National Portraits which have overflowed from the first-floor Galleries; and the rest of the room contains a more miscellaneous gathering, including Scottish Portrait Drawings; a series of Views of Old Edinburgh by the late James Drummond, R.S.A., lent from the National Museum of Antiquities; a series of Foreign Engraved Portraits, bequeathed by the late W. F. Watson; and a portion of the Albacini Collection of Plaster Casts from Antique Busts, the property of the Honourable the Board of Manufactures.

The two remaining Galleries on the top floor are similar in size to those below, but are separated from each other by a partition wall, instead of merely a series of open arches; and, being lighted from the roof, they present much wall-space for the display of portraits. At present only the northern Gallery is devoted to exhibition purposes. It contains a further selection from the Albacini Collection of Busts, and an interesting series of about two hundred engraved Scottish Portraits, bequeathed by W. F. Watson.

In addition to the Galleries in the main block, the western wing further contains several ample apartments, for the most

part stretching the full breadth of the edifice, and lighted from three sides. These will be eventually used for purposes of exhibition, and for the Library, Print Room, and Offices of the Portrait Gallery.

When we now turn to a consideration of the portraits which the buildings contain, we must restrict ourselves to the works which are either the property of the Gallery, or are deposited by private owners and by various public bodies upon loan for a lengthened and indefinite period ; omitting reference to those that have been lent for a short term only.

ROYAL PERSONAGES.

HE oldest of the portraits in the Gallery is that of King James V., the founder, in 1532, of the College of Justice, styled, for his affability and love of equity, the " King of the Poor." Traditions of his romantic adventures as he wandered through his country in disguise are familiar to readers of Scott's " Lady of the Lake," and form the subject of several of the old Scottish ballads, among the rest of " The Gaberlunzie Man " and " The Jolly Beggar," both attributed to the pen of the King himself, who in his childhood had been carried in the arms of Sir David Lindsay (see Illustration at the end of this Pamphlet), and soothed to sleep with the sound of that poet's lute and song. The portrait is an old picture on panel. In pose and costume it shows considerable resemblance to the figure of the monarch in the portrait at Hardwick, where he appears in company with his second Queen, Mary of Guise.

Of their still more celebrated daughter, Mary Queen of Scots, whose brief life in this country—it extended only from 1561 to 1568—has furnished an ever fascinating problem for the historian, a continually inspiring subject for the painter and the

NO. IV.

poet, the Gallery contains several interesting and authentic renderings. Perhaps the best of these is an electrotype from the head and bust of the recumbent alabaster statue, by Cornelius and William Cure, placed upon the tomb erected by her royal son over her grave in Westminster Abbey (Illustration No. V.) The tomb was commenced within nineteen years after his mother's death, and the face of the effigy must have been studied from the most authentic materials. The medal of Jacopo Primavera was probably executed in 1572, about the same time as that artist's medal of her cousin Queen Elizabeth which is hung beside it, a work cast in commemoration of the English monarch's recovery from small-pox in that year. Both medals are probably taken from painted portraits, for Primavera is not known to have ever been in England or Scotland, and Mr Cochran-Patrick believes the original of the medal of Mary to date from about 1566-7, when she was the wife of Darnley. Another very authentic type of Queen Mary's portraiture appears in the Gallery in an old copy from an original by Clouet, of which the drawing is preserved at Paris, and the oil picture in the Royal Collection at Windsor. This shows her as the widow of François II., dressed in the "*grand deuil blanc*" to which Brantôme refers in one of his poems.

Of Mary's son, James VI., the "Scottish Solomon," as he was styled for his erudition, in whose person the crowns of England and Scotland were united in 1603, the Gallery contains two portraits. One shows him as a round-cheeked chubby boy, in a red doublet, and with a black cap perched on his head. The other portrays him as a pale-faced, rather lethargic-looking man of twenty-nine, having been painted in 1595, about the time that he was engaged in his struggles with the Scottish clergy. His cousin, Lady Arabella Stuart, whose proximity to the crown made her life so bitter, and led to her imprisonment first by

Queen Elizabeth, and afterwards by James himself, we have a
curious old oval picture on panel, in which she appears holding
a lap-dog.   Passing to a much later date, Queen Anne, the
patriotic and resolute daughter of James VII. and Anne Hyde,
is portrayed by Sir Godfrey Kneller, clad in royal robes, wearing
the collar and jewel of the Garter, and holding the royal globe
and sceptre.

Of George II., the hero of Oudenarde and Dettingen, the
last sovereign of Great Britain who in person led his armies on
the field of battle, we have an imposing full-length gallery
picture, a signed example of John Shackleton, who in 1749 was
appointed principal painter to the King.   His stately Queen, the
wise, prudent, and long-suffering Caroline of Anspach, distinguished for her ability as a ruler, and for her patronage of
science and philosophy in the persons of Newton, Leibnitz, and
Butler, appears in a half-length by Jacopo Amigoni.   She is clad
in robes of state, and her right hand is very fittingly represented
resting on the crown, for of her, more than of most Queen
Consorts of England, it can be said that she was a true governor,
a real political force in the country.   During her husband's fre-
quent and prolonged absences at Hanover she acted as Regent,
and from the time of his accession till her own death in 1737 she
was his constant and most helpful adviser.

A gallery full-length, an important and excellent example of
the art of Allan Ramsay, portrays George III., who wore the
crown for all but sixty years, and was the first true Englishman
of the Hanoverian dynasty, the first sovereign of the line born
in Britain.   In a similar companion picture we have his Consort,
the good Queen Charlotte.   These two presentation state portraits formed part of the collection at Osmaston Hall, Derby.
George IV. is represented in a bust-portrait by Lawrence, from
an artistic point of view one of the finest works in the Gallery ;

and his Queen, wearing the broad hat and white ostrich plume of the period, is depicted in a half-length by Samuel Lane.

The series of royal portraits terminates with a bust of our beloved monarch Queen Victoria (Illustration No. VI.), by Sir John Steell, a work possessing much interest as having been executed from the life in 1838, the year of Her Majesty's accession, and being probably the earliest artistic rendering of her as Queen of Great Britain. Her Majesty's father, the Duke of Kent, appears in a bust by Turnerelli; while the Prince of Wales and his brother the Duke of Edinburgh are represented in busts by Steell.

POLITICAL AND LEGAL CELEBRITIES.

ONE of the earliest portraits in this class represents Archbishop James Sharp, who played such a shifty and feeble part in post-Restoration politics, and came to an evil end on Magus Moor. It is a half-length version of the well-known larger picture by Lely, engraved in Lodge's Portraits.

Another half-length, an old picture by an unknown artist, shows Lord President Sir George Lockhart, styled by Bishop Burnet "the best pleader I have ever known in any nation." He figured in many stirring scenes of national history; among the rest he defended Mitchell in his famous trial for the attempted assassination of Archbishop Sharp, and was also employed by Argyll at his trial. His death, in 1689, strikingly illustrates the dangerous condition of Scotland at the time, for, as will be remembered, he was shot as he was entering his house in the Old Bank Close, High Street, by John Chiesley of Dalry, in revenge for his having given decision against the murderer in a suit raised by his wife for aliment.

Sir Patrick Hume, first Earl of Marchmont—the tale of

whose hiding in the vault of Polwarth Church, where he was
supplied with food by his twelve-year-old daughter, the heroic
Grizel Baillie, forms one of the most picturesque episodes of
Scottish history—is from the brush of William Aikman, and
represents a mild-faced, white-bearded old man, in a long gown
and a soft blue cap, the troubles of his life now well over, and
succeeded by the peace of a tranquil age.

A contemporary portrait in water-colours, executed by
Joshua Campbell, at Elgin, "November 20th, 1746," the year
before its subject's death, represents the Right Hon. Duncan
Forbes of Culloden. His probity, wisdom, and dignity as Lord
President of the Court of Session, the powerful aid he rendered
to the Government during the Rebellion of 1745—expending
unstintingly his private fortune (which was never refunded)—
and his efforts in the direction of clemency and a conciliatory
policy when all public danger from the rising was over, entitle
him to a most honourable place among the effigies of Scotsmen
who have deserved well of their country.

Among later Scottish lawyers, Lord Rutherfurd, Solicitor-
General under the Melbourne Administration, appears in a full-
length by Watson Gordon, and in a sepia drawing by Crombie ;
the keen, critical, eminently practical face of Lord Jeffrey is
rendered in busts by Samuel Joseph and Sir John Steell, and in a
cabinet oil picture by Pairman ; while his friend and biographer,
Lord Cockburn, that most genial of Scottish Judges, whose
charming "Memorials" and "Journals" portray so vividly the
men and things of a past generation in our country, also figures in
an excellent bust by Steell, and in a characteristic full-length by
Watson Gordon. In the last-named picture he appears standing,
hat in hand, in the midst of a landscape whose distance shows
his beloved Pentland Hills, and, nestling at their foot, Bonaly
Tower, where he established himself on his marriage in 1811, and

which remained his cherished home for the rest of his life, for
over forty years. "Everything," he writes, "except the two
burns, the few old trees, and the mountains, are my own work,
and to a great extent the work of my own hands. Human
nature is incapable of enjoying more happiness than has been
my lot here." "Unless some avenging angel shall expel me, I
shall never leave that paradise."   .

The imposing figure of the Right Hon. David Boyle, Lord
President from 1841 to 1852, appears in a colossal full-length
statue by Sir John Steell; and from the same hand is a statue of
similar dimensions portraying James, Marquis of Dalhousie, so
celebrated while Governor-General of India for his successful
conduct of the great Sikh War, and of the second Burmese
War; for his annexation of the Punjab, Oudh, Pegu, and Nag-
pore; for his reorganisation of the Forest Department; for his
opening of the Civil Service to natives; and for the introduction
and carrying out of railways, telegraphs, canals, and many
public works.

Of the first Lord Melville, the most prominent and powerful
Scotsman of his day, the Gallery as yet contains in its permanent collection only two versions of the Tassie medallion;
but of his son, the second Viscount, First Lord of the Admiralty
in 1812, and again under the Wellington Administration of
1828, there is an important seated half-length by Colvin Smith;
while among later politicians, Sir James Gibson Craig appears
in a bust by Thomas Campbell; Sir William Gibson Craig is
painted by Watson Gordon; and the Right Hon. William
Dundas, Lord Clerk Register, by Hoppner.

MILITARY AND NAVAL MEN.

HE first exhibit under this class is a portrait of Oliver Cromwell, a great military leader and much besides, whose iron hand was felt so distinctly by the Scots in their defeat at Dunbar in 1650. The Lord Protector is portrayed in an old copy from the well-known figure in armour by Walker.

Field-Marshal Wade—Commander-in-Chief in Scotland after the Rebellion of 1715, and well known as the constructor of the roads and bridges which did so much to open up and civilise the Highlands—figures in a cabinet-sized full-length in oils, and in a pencil half-length sketched by Alexander Van Haecken for his contemporary mezzotint engraving after John Vanderbanck's painting.

Sir Ralph Abercromby, one of the very greatest of the military heroes of Scotland, is painted by Colvin Smith, in a full-length that is characteristic as a likeness, as may be seen by a comparison with the bust-portrait by Hoppner, engraved by S. W. Reynolds. This full-length, however, was not painted from the life, for Smith, born in 1795, was only six years of age when Abercromby fell, gloriously, at Alexandria.

Francis, first Marquis of Hastings, known as Lord Moira while Commander-in-Chief in Scotland, and afterwards celebrated in India, in a similar position and as Governor-General, by his operations against the Mahratta and Pindharee powers, and by his reforms in various departments of the public service, appears in a water-colour by J. S. Harvie; Major-General Sir Patrick Lindsay, another distinguished officer, is portrayed by Watson Gordon in his uniform, and wearing the Cross of the

Bath awarded him for his reduction
of Coorg in India; Lord Clyde, the
saviour of our Eastern Empire by
the relief of Lucknow in 1857, figures
in the very characteristic oil sketch,
done by Barker from the life in 1860,
which we reproduce as our Illustration No. VII.; and Admiral Viscount Duncan (Illustration No. VIII.)
in the vigorous medallion by Tassie.

NO. VIII.

ARTISTS.

AMONG the painters, the first names that we have
to mention are those of Alexander Runciman,
and his short-lived, but perhaps even more gifted
brother John Runciman. The former, best known
by his mural decorations in the Ossian Hall of Penicuik House,
appears in an oil picture, in company with his friend and
pupil, John Brown. Brown deserves a place in a Scottish
National Portrait Gallery for his successful efforts to preserve
the likeness of many distinguished Scotsmen. A series of
his pencil heads of the early members of the Society of Antiquaries of Scotland is hung in the present collection; and
these drawings are interesting no less on account of the delicate
beauty of their artistic method, than for the eminence of many
of the personages portrayed. They include David, Earl of
Buchan, the founder of the Society, by whom the series was
commissioned; William Smellie, the printer and botanist;
Adam Cardonnel, author of the "Numismata Scoticæ" and
"Picturesque Antiquities of Scotland;" George Paton, the
correspondent of Gough and Ritson; the—in his day—much-

abused Dr John Brown (1735-88), to whom we owe such medical reforms as the disuse of the lowering system in fevers ;
David Deuchar, the etcher and seal-engraver, from whom Sir
Henry Raeburn received his first hints in art ; and many another
Scotsman of note in his own time, and worthy of remembrance
still.   Other skilful drawings by the same hand portray the
learned and eccentric Lord Monboddo, the artist's especial
patron, and the friend of Burns, who celebrated the beauty and
charm of the judge's daughter ; Principal John Hunter of St
Andrews, an erudite editor of the classics ; and the Rev. John
Logan, the poet.

Another artist who has deserved well of the Portrait Gallery,
and whose likeness has found a place on the walls, is James
Tassie, painted, in fancy costume, by John Paxton.   Most widely
known by his reproductions of antique gems, the part of his
work in which he proved himself a capable original artist is his
extensive series of medallion portraits, including the heads of

NO. IX.

many of his most celebrated contemporaries, modelled, with a few excep-
tions, from the life ; a series which
may almost be said to do for the
Britain of the latter half of the
eighteenth century what the medallions of David d'Angers did for the
France of a somewhat later date.
Tassie modelled his heads in wax,
just as the great medallists of Italy
—Pisano, Pasti, Sperandio, and the
rest—did theirs ; and afterwards cast
them in a vitreous white enamel
paste, invented by himself and Dr Quin of Dublin, which
served instead of the bronze or lead that was the final

material of the fifteenth century medals. How extensive and
interesting this portion of Tassie's work is may be gathered by
a glance at the selection of about
seventy of his medallions of eminent
persons preserved in glass cases in
the Gallery. They include Robert
Foulis, the art-loving printer who
ruined himself by starting and main-
taining the "Foulis Academy" of
Glasgow, where Tassie was trained
as a modeller ; David Allan, Tassie's
fellow-pupil, the precursor of Wilkie
as a delineator of Scottish familiar
life ; Robert Adam, the architect,
from whom the Adelphi in London
is named ; David Hume, the historian (Illustration No. IX.);
Professors Black, Millar, James Gregory, Dugald Stewart
(Illustration No. X.), Cullen, Robi-
son, and Reid, Principal Robertson,
and a host of other personages not
less celebrated. In another section
we shall refer to his portraits of
Adam Smith ; but here we reproduce (Illustration No. XI.) a medallion of great interest, representing Sir
Henry Raeburn, one of the very few
extant likenesses of this greatest of
Scottish portrait-painters,—the bust
by Thomas Campbell, and the splendid
half-length in oils by his own hand,
are the only others known to us. This medallion has generally
been ranked as the work of Tassie : but the bold style of its

modelling, in, for example, such parts as the hair and the costume, recalls the vigorous handling—the "square touch"—
of Raeburn with the brush; and the traditions of the painter's family also point to its having been executed by his own hand.

The medallic portraiture of James Tassie was carried on, after his death in the last year of the eighteenth century, by his nephew and successor, William Tassie—it must be confessed with greatly diminished skill and artistic freedom; and in the works of John Henning, H.R.S.A., the art was continued till the middle of the present century. The Gallery contains examples of William Tassie's medallions, and also a good selection of medallions by Henning, the latter including contemporary heads of Sir Walter Scott, Professor Dugald Stewart, James Watt, the artist himself, and other Scotsmen of distinction. We reproduce, in Illustration No. XII., the portrait of David Dale, the great Glasgow manufacturer, whom Carlyle, in his characteristic letter on the subject, so emphatically pronounced worthy of a place in any Scottish National Portrait Gallery that might be formed.

Continuing our account of the portraits of painters included in the Gallery, we find two representing Allan Ramsay, son of the poet of the name, King's painter to George III., and a member of the most cultured London circles of his day. He was eulogised by Dr Johnson, who pronounced that "you will not find a man in whose conversation there is more instruction, more

information, and elegance, than in Ramsay's." Of the two portraits, that by his pupil, Alexander Nasmyth, is manifestly a
striking and faithful likeness.

Of David Martin—another of Ramsay's assistants, and,
indeed, his favourite pupil, who engraved several of his master's
portraits, that of David Hume in the National Gallery of Scotland among the rest, and himself painted some excellent works,
of which the portrait of Dr Cullen, belonging to the Royal
Medical Society, is a good example—we have a portrait by his
own hand ; the homely, earnest face of the great Sir David
Wilkie, R.A., appears in a picture by Beechey ; Wilkie's friend,
Andrew Geddes, excellent as a portrait-painter, still more
admirable as an etcher, appears in the small half-length by himself, which is engraved as the frontispiece of David Laing's
volume of " Etchings of Wilkie and Geddes ;" Sir Francis Grant,
the first and only Scotsman who has occupied the Presidential
chair of the Royal Academy, figures in a portrait by J. P. Knight;
and Horatio Macculloch, the well-known landscape-painter,
appears in a crayon drawing, and also in a somewhat similar
oil sketch, both by Sir Daniel Macnee. Two other celebrated
Scottish painters remain to be mentioned—Thomas Duncan,
one of Scotland's most notable figure-painters and colourists,
who is painted by Robert Scott Lauder, seated in meditative
attitude ; and Sir George Harvey, P.R.S.A., one of her most
successful landscape-painters, one of her most earnest painters
of scenes of national history and character, whom Mr J. Ballan-
tine has rendered, standing in the midst of his studio, busied in
front of his easel.

Architecture is represented by David Anderson, Dean of
Guild and apparently City Architect in Aberdeen at the end
of the sixteenth century, the designer of the steeple of St
Nicholas there ; by an Indian ink drawing of Sir William

Bruce, surveyor and master of the King's works to Charles II., the architect of Hopetoun House, and restorer in 1674 of Holyrood Palace; also, among more recent portraits, by George Meikle Kemp, the designer of the Scott Monument in Edinburgh, who is portrayed in a small oil picture by his relative William Bonnar, and in a bust by Handyside Ritchie.

In the department of Music, we have W. Smellie Watson's portrait of George Thomson, editor of that "Selection of Scottish Airs" in which Burns so materially assisted him; and, among executants, the celebrated Neil Gow, the most popular of Scottish violinists, appears, (Illustration No. XIII.) —seated in characteristic costume of blue coat and tartan hose, playing with a spirit all his own some reel or strath-spey—in the original portrait by Raeburn, which he after-wards several times repeated for various friends of the famous fiddler.

The representatives of Dramatic Art include William H. Murray, the well-known actor and Edinburgh manager, painted by Sir William Allan; his sister, Mrs Henry Siddons, the daughter-in-law of the great tragedienne, and a favourite of old Scottish play-goers; and Daniel Terry, who adapted several of the Waverley Novels for the stage, and who appears in a cabinet group by Geddes, in company with his wife, a daughter of Alexander Nasmyth, and herself known as a painter.

MEN OF LETTERS.

HE earliest of the Scottish men of letters who have found a place in the Gallery is Sir David Murray of Gorthy, Keeper of the Privy Purse to Prince Henry. His poems and translations were published by the Bannatyne Club in 1823. Bishop Burnet—who might fittingly have been referred to among the politicians, but figures here in virtue of the seventy volumes that he produced, including his valuable " History of My Own Times "—appears in two portraits, the most undoubtedly authentic being a small contemporary pencil drawing, full of character and delicacy. Dr Arbuthnot, better known as a satirist than as a medical man, though Swift—who eulogises him as possessing " as much wit as us all, and more humanity than wit "—calls him " Queen Anne's favourite physician," and we know that he attended that monarch on her death-bed, is portrayed in a signed portrait by William Robinson. Allan Ramsay, the shrewd, kindly author of " The Gentle Shepherd," to whose verse, and play-house, and circulating library the cause of culture in Scotland owes not a little, is as yet hardly represented with fitting prominence in the Gallery, which, however, contains a small oil portrait, a chalk sketch by Aikman, and a sepia drawing by Carse from the portrait by Smibert, now at Newhall, formerly in the poet's own possession and in his daughter's.

Dr Alexander Carlyle, whose " Autobiography," edited by Hill Burton, portrays so vividly the most celebrated of his eighteenth century contemporaries, appears in a characteristic oil portrait by Archibald Skirving ; where the face, with its aquiline features and long snowy locks, amply realises Sir Walter's description of the minister of Inveresk as "a grand old

carl," and recalls the story of the sculptor who stopped him in
the London streets, and asked him to sit for a head of "Jupiter"
—a majestic title which, ever after, clung to the good old clergy-
man.

Henry Mackenzie, author of "The Man of Feeling," and
one of the first appreciative reviewers of Burns, is figured,
in the emaciation of extreme old age, in a very striking marble
bust by Joseph. Dr M'Crie, author of the "Life of Knox,"
and of much else of value, appears in the important portrait
by Watson Gordon, well known, in its engraved form, as the
frontispiece of his works. Dr Thomas Henry, the author of
a history of Scotland, celebrated in its day and praised by
Hume, is seen in clerical gown and wig in an oil picture by
Martin; and two later and better-known historians of our
country, Patrick Fraser Tytler and John Hill Burton, appear
in the Gallery—the former in a cabinet-sized version of the
portrait by Watson Gordon, the latter in a marble bust executed by Alexander Rhind after that modelled from the life,
in 1859, by Brodie.

One of the most important works in the Gallery, both
from its interest as a national portrait and its excellence as
a work of art, is Raeburn's full-length of Professor John
Wilson, which we reproduce as our Illustration No. XIV., a
picture painted about 1805, portraying the author of the
"Isle of Palms," the genial "Christopher North" of the
"Noctes," in all the vigour of his splendid early manhood.
This is one of the pictures that are the property of the
Royal Scottish Academy and have been transferred from the
National Gallery.

Thomas Campbell, an author less read than he once was,
though certain of his direct and powerful lyrics will always
hold their place in our literature, is painted in a half-length

by Henry Room, dated 1841, three years before the poet's death ; and among minor Scottish bards we have a unique and admirable bust, by his master Chantrey, of " Honest Allan" Cunningham, almost the single man of letters in London who seems to have commanded Carlyle's very considerable respect ; while Motherwell's well-conditioned features are preserved in a bust by James Fillans ; and William Tennant—author of " Anster Fair," and known, too, as an Orientalist and author of a " Syrian and Chaldaic Grammar" —figures in a small water-colour by an unknown hand.

Passing to literary men who have been our own recent contemporaries, the rugged face of Thomas Carlyle, worn and wearied with the strenuous and unceasing effort of his life—that " battle " which all his authorship so truly was —looks out upon us from a bust by Brodie, (Illustration No. XV.) ; Dean Ramsay, the wide-hearted Churchman and compiler of the immensely popular " Reminiscences of Scottish Life and Character," is portrayed—from personal recollection, not directly from the sitter—in a bust by Sir John Steell ; while of Dr John Brown, the genial author of " Rab and His Friends," a man beloved by thousands, on both sides of the Atlantic, who have seen, and who have never seen, his face in life, we have the best of existing portraits, the vivid oil sketch by Mr George Reid, reproduced as our Illustration No. XVI.

The names of the two greatest of Scottish writers—and these not the greatest only, but also the most typically Scottish —still remain to be mentioned ; and the Gallery is fortunate in possessing authentic and interesting portraits of both Burns and Scott.

The most adequate and important of all the renderings of Burns is, of course, the bust portrait in oils by Alexander

Nasmyth, of which the original version, painted from life, hangs in the National Gallery of Scotland; while two other versions, also by Nasmyth's hand, are in the National Portrait Gallery, London, and at Auchendrane, Ayrshire. In the Scottish National Portrait Gallery, however, is the interesting seated portrait by Peter Taylor; a work executed from the life, as is amply proved by the testimony of those who knew the circumstances and the sitter well; and doubtless preserving much that was ordinarily characteristic of the great bard of Scotland. The Gallery also contains the silhouette portrait of Burns which is repeatedly referred to in his letters; and in the collection of Engraved Scottish Portraits the Burns' items include Beugo's small engraving, executed from Nasmyth's picture, but supplemented with touches from the life—for the poet gave his friend the engraver the advantage of sittings during the progress of the plate, and also Walker's engraving from the same picture, (Illustration No. XVII.), of which the painter said, "It conveys to me a more true and lively remembrance of Burns than my own picture does, it so perfectly renders the spirit of his expression, as well as the details of his every feature." The marble statue by Flaxman, in the Central Hall below, is not from life, and may be regarded rather as part of the decoration of the Gallery than of its Portrait Collection proper.

Of Sir Walter Scott the series of portraits is more extensive, ranging from his first miniature as a child to the last portrait, painted the year before his death.

The earliest portrait we reproduce as Illustration No. XVIII. It is known as "The Bath Miniature," and was painted for Scott's mother; but, having become broken, as is visible in our plate, a copy was executed from it, and the original, presented to a friend, was eventually acquired by David Laing, and has passed into

the National Collection.   It shows a delicate, earnest, enquiring
face, with long, curling, light-brown hair; and the profile, with

its long upper lip and high forehead,
is curiously little altered in the bust
modelled by Chantrey in 1820, of
which a cast is in the Gallery.   Here,
too, are the medallion by Henning,
modelled in 1809, the year after the
publication of "Marmion;" the delicate head by Andrew Geddes, dating
from about 1818; a slight pencil outline by the Russian artist Ströling;
and the full-length sepia drawing by
Crombie, showing the "Wizard of   no. xviii.
the North" standing in the midst of
one of the Scottish landscapes over which his works have shed
the light of a new enchantment.

But most pathetic of all is that last portrait of Scott in his
study (Illustration No. XIX.), painted by Sir Francis Grant
in 1831, when, with broken health and enfeebled powers, the
great novelist was at work on "Count Robert of Paris."   The
picture, pronounced by its subject "far better than Watson's,
though that too was well," was commissioned by Lady Ruthven,
from whom it passed directly to the Gallery; and the circumstances attending its execution are preserved in a letter by
the painter, published in the Catalogue of the Scott Centenary
Exhibition.

CLERGYMEN.

EVERAL clergymen have already been included among the names of men famous in literature ; but the Gallery also contains the effigies of some who have achieved fame in more purely professional ways. The Rev. Dr John Inglis, of whom we have a life-sized half-length in oils, was chiefly known by his appearances in the General Assembly, as the head, during many years, of the "Moderate" party, and by his exertions in the promotion of Indian Missions. The Rev. Archibald Alison, whose refined face is preserved in a bust by Joseph, was famous equally as a preacher and an essayist ; Dr Chalmers, portrayed in a bust by Sir John Steell, is even more significant as an ecclesiastical figure than as a writer on economics and astronomy ; Dr Lindsay Alexander, painted by Norman Macbeth, was distinguished in the pulpit hardly less than in the study, where his eminence as a scholar procured him a place on the Old Testament Revision Committee ; Dr Thomas Guthrie, who appears in a little known but highly characteristic bronze head by Sir John Steell, is best remembered as a fervid orator and an effective philanthropist ; and the Rev. Principal Tulloch, represented in one of the very latest examples of Herdman's brush, was a leader in the Church courts and an academic teacher, as well as a prolific author.

METAPHYSICIANS, ECONOMISTS, PHILOLOGISTS.

MONG the metaphysicians, the homely aged face of Dr Thomas Reid, the eminent author of the "Inquiry into the Human Mind" and of the essays on "The Active and Intellectual Powers of Man," is present in one of the versions of Raeburn's painting. His biographer and his editor are also included in the Gallery— Professor Dugald Stewart figuring in a metal bust by Joseph, and Sir William Hamilton, the most celebrated of recent Scottish metaphysicians, in an oil portrait by Mr J. Ballantyne.

At the head of our political economists stands Adam Smith. We reproduce one of the two medallions by Tassie (Illustration No. XX.), which, with the exception of the etchings executed by Kay just after their subject's death, and probably studied from the medallions, are the only authentic renderings of the author of "The Wealth of Nations." The medallion here given represents him in a curled wig and the costume of the period; the other is executed in what the modeller, in the catalogue of his works, calls "the antique manner," that is to say, with the subject wearing his own hair, and with no drapery appearing over the bust. The estimable and accomplished Francis Horner may also most fittingly be ranked with the economists. He is represented in an admirable example of the portraiture of Raeburn, which forms a curious pictorial comment on that fine pen-portrait of its subject drawn

No. XX.

by Sidney Smith :—" There was something very remarkable in his countenance—the commandments were written on his face, and I have often told him there was not a crime he might not commit with impunity, as no judge or jury who saw him would give the smallest degree of credit to any evidence against him."

Among the students of philology, the Rev. John Jamieson, the compiler of that monumental work, the " Scottish Dictionary," holds a high place.   He is depicted in an excellent little cabinet picture by Yellowlees.   A pencil drawing by Andrew Geddes portrays Professor Alexander Murray, author of " Outlines of Oriental Philology," and of a " History of European Languages." The Rev. Professor Andrew Dalzel appears, clad in academic gown and seated in a red arm-chair, in a three-quarter length by Raeburn.   Professor of Greek in the University of Edinburgh, he was a philologist, and much more, for he stirred in his pupils an enthusiasm for both Greek thought and life.   Lord Cockburn, one of his pupils, has left in his " Memorials" very attractive reminiscences of Dalzel's appearance in his class.

We reproduce, as our Illustration No. XXI., a telling three-quarter length of Dr William Veitch, a genial and learned scholar of our own day (he died in 1885), who devoted himself to purely textual criticism with an exclusiveness rare indeed in Scotland, and whose " Greek Verbs, Irregular and Defective," is a work too well known and esteemed to require further mention.   The painting is by James Irvine, and ranks as one of the most successful examples of his brush.

MEN OF SCIENCE.

AMONG the students of physical science, and those who have applied the powers of nature to the service of man, we find in the Gallery a good representation of James Watt, inventor of the expansion steam-engine, investigator of the composition of water. He figures in the well-known bust modelled by Chantrey, and also in the bust-sized drawing in crayons by Henning which we reproduce as Illustration No. XXII., evidently a study for its artist's small medallion portrait of which a cast is preserved in one of the glass cases. The look of quiet concentration, the meditative and cautious expression, which is so markedly present in all these portraits of Watt, is also characteristic of another of Scotland's mechanical geniuses, Robert Stevenson, the lighthouse builder, as rendered in a cast of the bust, by Joseph, at the Bell Rock. By the same sculptor is the bust of Professor Sir John Leslie, the investigator of the laws of heat, the inventor of the Differential Thermometer and the Hydrometer, a work reproduced in marble by Mr John Rhind from Joseph's contemporary plaster. Mathematics are represented by Professor Playfair, who appears in William Nicholson's sepia study for his etched portrait, and in an especially sensitive and delicately - modelled head of Chantrey ; Mrs Somerville, astronomer and mathematician, the one eminent Scottish woman of science, appears in a medallion by Robert Macpherson ; while the keen shaven face of Professor Edward Forbes, the geologist, with its thin features and sharply aquiline nose, looks out, in the bust by Sir John Steell, from the flakes of long lank hair that surround it.

. The Gallery contains portraits of several of the self-taught men of science of whom Scotland has always been proud. The

earliest of these, portrayed in a coloured crayon drawing, is James Ferguson, the shepherd-boy who trained himself to be an astronomer.   The vigorous, determined face, with its large features and resolute lips, of Hugh Miller, the famous Cromarty mason, author of "Old Red Sandstone," and "The Testimony of the Rocks," is sympathetically rendered in a bust by Brodie. Like Charles Maclaren, the geologist and editor of the *Scotsman*, who appears in a marble bust by Brodie after Hutchison, Miller might figure either in the present section as a man of science, or among the representatives of letters, as a journalist and editor of the *Witness*.   Thomas Edward, the cobbler field-naturalist, whose enthusiasm for science no hardships could extinguish, and whose career has been sketched in so fascinating a manner by Dr Samuel Smiles, is represented in a spirited sketch made by Mr George Reid from his oil-picture done from life.

The series of Scottish travellers opens with the highly-finished oil-portrait, which forms our Illustration No. XXIII., of James Bruce of Kinnaird, the earliest of celebrated Scottish explorers, author of the well-known "Travels to Discover the Sources of the Nile."   Captain Hugh Clapperton, who is portrayed in a small water-colour, merits a place by his African expeditions, which finally cost his life ; and Sir John Ross, the Arctic explorer and companion of Parry, appears in an oil half-length by B. R. Faulkner.

Representative of medical science in Scotland, we have a bust of Alexander Monro, M.D., the second member of the distinguished family that founded, and for over a hundred years— father, son, and grandson—held the Chair of Anatomy in the Edinburgh University.   Not only was he an able professor and medical author, but he is also styled by Dr James Gregory "the very ideal of a practical physician and consultant."   Of Dr Gregory himself, a no less celebrated professor in the same

university, the best rendering in the Gallery is the dignified and individual bust by Joseph ; and of Dr Andrew Duncan, *primus*, his successor as Professor of the Theory of Medicine, and the founder and helper of many good works in Edinburgh, the most important rendering is an oil-painting by Martin. Among the chemists, Dr Cullen figures in an exceedingly quaint and characteristic drawing by David Allan ; and Dr Joseph Black, the discoverer of "fixed air," or "carbonic acid gas," is represented in a coloured crayon portrait by an unknown hand.

ANTIQUARIES.

ENTION has already been made, in our account of the artists represented in the Gallery, of the series of pencil drawings by John Brown representing the founders of the Society of Antiquaries of Scotland ; but the Gallery also contains several portraits of later Scottish antiquaries. Among these are the oil portraits, by John Irvine and Thomas Fraser, of Charles Kirkpatrick Sharpe, the fastidious and curious collector, styled by Sir Walter Scott "the Scottish Walpole," the pungent editor of old-world literature, the witty etcher and caricaturist, in whose recently-published "Correspondence" will be found many strange records of a past state of society. Thomas Thomson, brother of the celebrated painter-minister of Duddingston, and editor of the valuable edition of the Scottish Acts of Parliament and of much else of antiquarian interest, is portrayed in an oil picture by Robert Scott Lauder ; and David Laing, the most celebrated of all the antiquaries of our country, who has done more than any other man to further the study of early Scottish literature, and to whose bequest the Gallery owes several

interesting items, is depicted in a bust modelled from recollection by Mr D. W. Stevenson, and in an oil portrait from the life, by Herdman, which represents its subject surrounded by the ancient volumes that he loved, collected, and reprinted, and amid which he laboured all his life.

J. M. GRAY,
Curator.

OPENING OF THE SCOTTISH NATIONAL PORTRAIT GALLERY.

(Revised from *Scotsman* of 16th July 1889.)

N the presence of a large, influential, and representative company of ladies and gentlemen, the Marquis of Lothian, K.T., Secretary for Scotland, yesterday formally opened the new Scottish National Portrait Gallery, erected in Queen Street, Edinburgh, by the generosity of a private donor, whose name up till then had remained a profound secret. The disclosure of the identity of the "anonymous donor," which took place in the course of the programme, lent additional interest and *éclat* to the proceedings. The ceremony was held in the lower gallery, which had been suitably prepared for the occasion. At a quarter to four o'clock the Secretary for Scotland took the chair, accompanied to the platform by the Trustees of the Board of Manufactures, and other gentlemen, among whom were :—

The Earl of Glasgow, the Lord Justice-General, Lord Provost Boyd, Edinburgh ; Sir James King, Lord Provost of Glasgow ; Lord Shand, Lord Kinnear, Principal Sir William Muir, the Hon. Bouverie Primrose, Sir William Walker, Chairman of the Board of Supervision ; Sir Thomas Jamieson Boyd, Chairman of the Fishery Board ; Sir Arthur Mitchell, Mr J. Ritchie Findlay, Major-General Sir R. Murdoch Smith, Sir Arthur Halkett, Bart. ; Sir William Fettes Douglas, Mr J. G. Maconochie Welwood, Mr John Cowan of Beeslack, Dr Rowand Anderson, architect ; Mr Gourlay Steell, R.S.A., Curator, National Gallery of Scotland ; Mr J. M. Gray, Curator, Scottish National Portrait Gallery, &c.

The general company included the following ladies and
gentlemen :—

The Earl of Ancrum, the Lord Justice-Clerk, Lord Adam, Mrs and Miss
Adam, Lord Kyllachy, Lord Lee, Mrs and Miss Lee, Lord M'Laren, Mrs
and Miss M'Laren, Lord Trayner, Mrs and Miss Trayner, the President of
the Faculty of Actuaries, Mrs Boyd, Lady King, Sir William and Lady
Morier, Lady Boyd, Lady Walker and the Misses Walker, General and Mrs
Dalyell, General Hope, Colonel Malcolm, R.E. ; Commander Dundas, Major
Leslie, Major-General Anderson, C.B., and Miss Anderson ; Sir William
Turner, Mrs J. R. Findlay, Mr J. L. Findlay, and the Misses Findlay ; Miss
Flora Clift Stevenson, Lady Clerk and the Misses Clerk, Lady Foulis, Lady
Halkett, Miss Halkett, Lady Macnee, Honourable Mrs Dundas, Miss Dundas,
Miss L. D. Dundas, Honourable Mrs Patrick Blair, Sheriff-Substitute
Orphoot, Sheriff Crichton, Professor Crum Brown, Professor Copeland, Pro-
fessor Duff, Chairman of the Edinburgh School Board ; Professor J. C. Ewart,
Professor A. C. Fraser, Professor Geikie, Professor Sir Douglas Maclagan
and Miss Maclagan, Professor Masson, Professor Mackinnon, Principal
Peterson, Professor Rankine, Professor Simpson, Dr Peel Ritchie, Rev. Dr
Adamson, Dr Joseph Anderson, Dr James Burgess, Dr Christison, Dr James
Foulis, Rev. Dr Goold, Dr and Mrs Keith, Mr Law, Miss Cameron, Mr
George Harrison Law, Rev. Dr Cameron Lees, Mr Charles A. Cooper, Dr
Munro, Dr and Miss Potts, Dr Paterson, Dr Argyll Robertson and Mrs
Robertson, Dr and Mrs Steele, Dr Grainger Stewart, Rev. Dr Taylor,
Rev. Mr Burns, Professor Flint, Rev. Mr Ritchie, Provost Aitken, Leith ;
Provost Keir, Musselburgh ; Bailies M'Donald, Russell, and Walcot ;
Treasurer Clapperton, Councillors Colston, Kinloch Anderson, Crighton,
Gibson, Gulland, Hogg, M'Intosh, Maclaren, Miller, Paterson, James Robert-
son, Tait, Turnbull ; the Mayor of South Shields ; Messrs P. W. Adam,
A.R.S.A. ; J. Denovan Adam, A.R.S.A. ; Robert Adam, City Chamberlain ;
Mr and Mrs Stair Agnew ; Messrs Robert Gibb, R.S.A., George Hay, R.S.A.,
John Hutchison, R.S.A. ; Mr and Mrs T. G. Murray ; Mr Wm. M'Taggart,
R.S.A. ; Mr W. D. M'Kay, R.S.A. ; Mr Erskine Nicol, R.S.A. ; Mr F. Noël
Paton, Mr George Reid, R.S.A. ; Mr Clark Stanton, R.S.A. ; Mr and Mrs
Skelton, Mr Gillies Smith, Mr J. Irvine Smith, Mr Lockhart Thomson, Mr
Spencer Thomson, Mr Usher of Norton, Mr W. F. Vallance, R.S.A., &c.

The SECRETARY FOR SCOTLAND said—My Lords, Ladies,
and Gentlemen, we have met upon an occasion of very great
interest, not only to Edinburgh, but to the whole of Scotland ;
but as I am going to ask you a little later on to allow me to
inflict a few words upon you, I shall not say more at present

than this, that a great number of apologies have been received
from representatives of all classes in Scotland of those who are
unable to be present to-day, but who have, nevertheless, shown
a very great interest in our proceedings. I have, first of all, to
call upon the Lord Justice-General, who is desirous of making a
few remarks to you.

The LORD JUSTICE-GENERAL said—My Lords, Ladies, and
Gentlemen, I have been requested by my colleagues of the
Board of Manufactures to offer you some explanation of what,
for want of a better name, I may call the genesis of the National
Portrait Gallery which is to be opened this day by our noble
Chairman. The patriotic sentiment which underlies and prompts
the desire of men in this country to possess authentic pictorial
representations of the great and notable men and women of
Scotland has not its origin in late days, nor is it in any way of
factitious creation. It is, indeed, part of the national character.
So early as the year 1778 two very remarkable men entered into
a correspondence upon this subject, which has fortunately been
preserved—I mean that distinguished antiquarian and historian
Lord Hailes, and that not less prominent and distinguished Scotsman, David, Earl of Buchan. They were at that time engaged
in laying the foundations of the Society of Scottish Antiquaries,
by whose zeal, learning, and industry has been erected that
splendid Museum of National Antiquities, the property of which
was transferred more than thirty years ago by the Society to the
Board of Manufactures in trust for the nation, and is soon to be
housed under the same roof with the National Portrait Gallery.
This happy conjunction fully realises and justifies the original
conception of Lord Hailes and the Earl of Buchan that National
Antiquities and National Portraiture have a natural if not a
necessary connection. Their ambition at that time did not extend
beyond a collection of engraved portraits ; and the outcome of it

all was the two publications by Mr Pinkerton, which are very
well known—the *Iconographica Scotica*, and the *Scottish Gallery*
—which contain a number of engraved portraits, the engravings
certainly not being of a very high class, but valuable because
they are chiefly drawn from what are well known and authentic
pictures, although, I must say at the same time, mingled with
some which are of very doubtful or spurious origin. The next
event to which I would venture to allude is the correspondence
between two other very distinguished Scotsmen—Thomas Carlyle and David Laing—which took place in 1854, upon the same
subject, both of them entering into it with great enthusiasm.
There is a letter by Mr Carlyle which is so much to the point,
and at the same time so characteristic of the writer, that I make
no apology for reading to you two or three extracts from it.   It
is addressed to Mr Laing. He says—" In all my poor Historical
investigations it has been, and always is, one of the most primary
wants to procure a bodily likeness of the personage inquired
after ; a good *Portrait*, if such exists ; failing that, even an indifferent if sincere one.   In short, *any* representation, made by a
faithful human creature, of that Face and Figure, which *he* saw
with his eyes, and which I can never see with mine, is now valuable to me, and much better than none at all. . . . Often I have
found a Portrait superior in real instruction to half a dozen
written ' Biographies,' as Biographies are written—or rather, let
me say, I have found that the Portrait was as a small lighted
candle by which the Biographies could for the first time be *read*,
and some human interpretation be made of them ; the *Biographied*
Personage no longer an empty impossible Phantasm, or distract-
ing Aggregate of inconsistent rumours—(in which state, alas ! his
usual one, he is *worth* nothing to anybody, except it be as a
dried thistle for Pedants to thrash, and for men to fly out of the
way of)—but yielding at last some features which one could

admit to be human." He goes on further to say—"It has always struck me that Historical Portrait Galleries far transcend in worth all other kinds of National Collections of Pictures whatever; that, in fact, they ought to exist (for many reasons, of all degrees of weight) in every country as among the most popular and cherished National Possessions—and it is not a joyful reflection, but an extremely mournful one, that in no country is there at present such a thing to be found." It must be remembered that this was in the year 1854. Finally, he says—"I hope you in Scotland, in the 'new National Museum' we hear talk of, will have a good eye to this, and remedy it in your own case. Scotland at present is not worse than other countries in the point in question, but neither is it at all better; and as Scotland, unlike some other countries, *has* a History of a very readable nature, and has never published even an *engraved* series of National Portraits, perhaps the evil is more sensible and patent there than elsewhere. It is an evil which should be everywhere remedied; and if Scotland be the first to set an example in that respect, Scotland will do honourably by herself, and achieve a benefit to all the world." Mr Laing took what may without offence be called a somewhat more sober-minded view of the subject, and in presenting this letter to the Society of Antiquaries, of which he was a distinguished member, he dilated rather on the difficulties of the undertaking and the great expense; for he says—"It is with no intention of proposing that the Society should undertake this that I have brought it under their notice. To be successfully launched would require the influence and the means of the. Honourable Board of Trustees, possessing apartments most suitable for the purpose." At that time, I am sorry to say, the Board of Trustees were not in a position to undertake so very serious and costly an enterprise. They were possessed, no

doubt, of galleries admirably fitted for the exhibition of national
portraits, but unfortunately they were all appropriated to other
equally important objects ; and although there was a vague sus-
picion in the public mind that the Board of Manufactures was a
rich body, they were unfortunately only rich in this sense, that they
administered a certain amount of public moneys which were all
appropriated to specific purposes, and therefore they had no
means of undertaking anything like the creation of a National
Portrait Gallery. However, the subject became one of great
interest from various events which occurred not long after the
time that I am now speaking of. In the first place, the Portrait
Gallery of London was opened in the year 1859, and in that same
year there was a very attractive exhibition in Aberdeen of portraiture, chiefly confined to the neighbourhood of that city. In
Glasgow, again, in 1868, there was a similar exhibition of portraits ; and the loan exhibitions of South Kensington, which I
dare say many of you have some recollection of, were opened in
the years 1866, 1867, and 1868. It thus became pretty obvious
that Scottish national portraiture was in the air, and that something must be done. But how long we might have waited for
that something to come about, it is very difficult to tell, if it had
not been that the Board of Manufactures received unexpected,
but most valued aid from a private quarter. (Applause.)

In 1882, on the 7th December, they had a communication made
to them from my friend Sir William Fettes Douglas, the President
of the Scottish Academy, that a gentleman, whose name was in
the meantime not disclosed, was willing to give £10,000 to help
to make an endowment for a collection of national portraits, if an
equal amount could be had from public sources. I am happy to
say that the Treasury gave an equal sum in the following year,
and so the Board were at last put in possession of means to com-
mence the purchase and collection of national portraits. The

gentleman who had made this gift suggested, very properly, to
the Board of Manufactures, for the purpose of stimulating
interest in the subject, that they should open a loan exhibition in
one of their galleries, and this was done in 1883, and afterwards
in 1884, the exhibition of 1883 being divided almost equally
between national portraits and pictures by the old masters, and a
very attractive exhibition it undoubtedly was. In 1884 the
exhibition consisted entirely of national portraits, and I venture
to read to you, in connection with it, a sentence from the preface
to the catalogue of the exhibition of 1884, which will give you
some information of how that exhibition was got up. It says :
—" The present loan exhibition of portraits of eminent Scottish
men and women, and of persons intimately connected with Scotland, has been brought together by the Board of Trustees for
Manufactures in Scotland, in anticipation of the opening of the
permanent Scottish National Portrait Gallery, with the view of
interesting the public in the subject of portraiture generally, and
of ascertaining the present resting-places of important works of
this class in the country. It is believed that, taken in connection with the portrait department of last autumn's exhibition,
the present collection will afford a not inadequate view of Scottish portraiture, and that it will give valuable opportunities for
study and comparison." I think I am not speaking in a spirit of
too great self-complacency when I say on behalf of the Board
that these exhibitions were highly successful, and did create a
vast amount of interest in the subject with which we are now
dealing.

But the only gallery in which it was possible for the Board
of Manufactures to house the portraits which they had begun
to collect was, unfortunately, occupied by another important
institution—the Society of Scottish Antiquaries. The Royal
Institution on the Mound, as you are well aware, had at that

time, and has still, its principal room entirely occupied by their
Museum. Of course, it was proposed that the Museum should be
removed to another public building, and it was all the more desirable that this should be done because the space allotted to it
in the Royal Institution was quite inadequate for the exhibition
of their treasures. But great difficulties occurred, and, as was
natural, the Society of Scottish Antiquaries were somewhat hard
to please. I do not blame them, considering the extreme value
of the treasures under their charge. It was not at all an easy
matter to find in any other public building accommodation that
would satisfy them. Now, it was at this critical moment that
our valued friend, although he still continued anonymous,
stepped in to the rescue again, and offered the sum of £20,000—
(loud applause)—to erect a building which should be capable of
providing accommodation for the Society of Antiquaries as well
as for a National Portrait Gallery. (Applause.) Thus armed
with an endowment, and with the prospect of a building, everything appeared to the Board in rose colour. But I dare say all
who hear me are aware that estimates for building are very
shifty things—(laughter)—and that when you begin to build you
require to count the cost upon a rather extravagant scale. Well,
the end of it all is that our anonymous donor has provided, first
and last, including the £10,000 which he gave for the endowment originally, a sum of £50,000, which he has placed in the
hands of the Board of Manufactures. (Applause.) Gentlemen,
it is difficult to speak without some extravagance of language
upon the munificence of this generous gift, but I am sure you
will all agree with me that the thanks, not only of the Board of
Manufactures, but of the whole people of Scotland, are due to
that gentleman for the extremely well-timed, as well as munificent, gift which he has made. (Loud applause.) You have this
day to a certain extent seen the result of this munificence. You

are assembled in a building which, I think, when you have seen more of it than you have yet, you will pronounce to be extremely well adapted for the purpose for which it has been erected. When completed, I think I may venture to say that there will not be a finer building in the city of Edinburgh, or perhaps in Scotland. (Applause.) The architect, in designing this building, as an architect always should do in designing any kind of building, took into account, first, what was the nature and the extent of the accommodation required, and then he considered what was the best style of architecture to secure that amount of accommodation. The accommodation required was of a nature which you can easily now understand, and the style of architecture which he adopted was, in his own words, "the secular Gothic of the latter half of the thirteenth century, a style that lends itself readily to the purpose of the building, and secures the greatest amount of light to those rooms that must be lighted from the side only."

There is one detail in connection with the design of this building as to which I should like to say a word, and that is the niches which are left all round for statues. There is no doubt, I think, that the union of sculpture and architecture is most desirable. It is much too little studied, I think, in this country; and, in regard to this particular building, it surely would be most appropriate that these niches should be filled with statues of eminent Scotsmen of times past. (Applause.) The difficulty in a case of this kind is to make a start. Who is to be the first donor of a statue? Because I need hardly tell you that we look to you and the people of Scotland generally to provide these; but I will venture to say from my own personal knowledge, that if we had once made a beginning—once got the first statue erected, I know it will be followed by others. (Applause.) With regard to the contents of the Gallery which you are pre-

sently to be introduced to, I may give you this information
generally—and it is not necessary to go into any detail—that
the pictures and busts for the most part are the property of the
Board ; but there are also a considerable number of pictures
which we have upon loan from noblemen and gentlemen, who
have been extremely generous and obliging, not only now, but
in former times when we had our exhibitions in 1883 and 1884 ;
and we have felt very strongly that a great deal of the success
both of these exhibitions and of the opening of the present
exhibition will be due to the generosity of these private indivi-
duals. I think it is perhaps no small reason for congratulation
that from the first subscription of the £10,000 by our munificent
donor only seven years have elapsed, and here we are with a
Portrait Gallery well hung. It affords a pretty strong contrast
to the adventures of the London Portrait Gallery, which has been
described by some of its warmest friends as " leading a vaga-
bond life for thirty years." (Laughter.) But I very much
rejoice to know, as I am sure you will also, that that collection at last is to have an adequate and permanent resting-place,
and, oddly enough, by the very same means by which we have
secured ours—the intervention of an anonymous donor. (Applause.) We have had, however, our period of nomadic life, and
I am very happy to take this occasion of returning thanks to the
Senatus Academicus of the University of Edinburgh for the
handsome way in which they took us in—I mean in the most
honourable and most hospitable sense of the word. (Laughter.)
The pictures were housed there for some considerable time in
rooms which, fortunately, were not immediately required for the
purposes of the University, and so they have been kept out of
harm's way, and are now, I think, to be presented to you this
afternoon in the highest possible condition. I cannot help going
back once more to the gift of our anonymous friend. I think

the great distinguishing feature of that gift is that it is entirely
national in its purposes, in its aims, and in its results ; and in
that respect I cannot recall—I may be wrong—any gift of at
all the same amount that has ever been made for purely and
thoroughly national purposes. That, I think, is the distinctive
character of this gift which gives it so much importance and so
much value. It was not to be wondered at that this gift and the
use made of it should attract a great deal of public attention,
and that there should be many speculations as to who was the
anonymous donor, and a great deal of curiosity—and investiga-
tion, I might almost say—(laughter), for the purpose of finding
out the well-kept secret. But I am happy to tell you that
speculation is now to come to an end—(loud applause)—that
curiosity is to be satisfied, and the donor is to stand face to face
before you. (Renewed applause.) He is a distinguished citizen
of Edinburgh, given to all manner of good works, an intelligent
lover of art, a zealous archæologist, and a Commissioner of
the Board of Manufactures. (Applause.) If that seems like a
conundrum, I can only say I think it is one of easy solution, and
you must, I think, all have arrived by this time at the conclusion
that the donor is Mr John Ritchie Findlay. (Loud and continued applause.)

The SECRETARY FOR SCOTLAND said he had now to call upon
Mr Findlay to speak a few words to them. (Applause.)

Mr J. R. FINDLAY, who was received with applause, said—
Lord Lothian, my Lords, Ladies and Gentlemen, it seems to be
my duty now, however imperfectly I may discharge it, to endeavour to thank you for your kind reception of the mention of my
name by my right hon. friend the Lord Justice-General. Persons who find themselves in such a position as that which I now
occupy before this distinguished assemblage are, I find from a
careful study of newspaper reports, very apt to say that they

cannot express their feelings, and then they immediately begin
to attempt to do what they have just pronounced to be impossible. I am inclined to think that it will be much easier and
pleasanter for both of us if I leave you to imagine my feelings than
if I were to attempt to express them. But, it may be asked,
Why, then, do you appear at all? Well, in the first place, I am
not primarily here as the "anonymous donor," of whom so much
has been said, but as a member of the Board of Manufactures ;
in the second place, I had a natural desire to be present on such
an interesting occasion, and I did not very well see why I should
not gratify that desire—(applause)—and, in the third place, as I
knew that the Lord President was going to let the cat out of the
bag, I thought it would be rather cowardly not to face it out.
At this moment I am inclined to wish that I had had less
temerity and more prudence. (Laughter.) It would be mere
mock modesty on my part, and not complimentary to you, were
I not frankly to declare that this is a very proud day in my life.
(Applause.) I am proud of your approbation ; I am proud to
witness the happy inauguration of a project which you so
emphatically approve ; and I am also proud to see what was long
with me a mere day-dream take concrete shape in the institution
so handsomely housed in this building.

The conviction that Scotland ought to have a National
Portrait Gallery had haunted me long before I had the faintest
idea that I could ever help to realise it. I have lived con-
siderably more than half a century in Edinburgh, and Edinburgh has been very good to me in every way. I have taken
this mode of showing my gratitude. (Loud applause.) But
if in the month of August 1833, when I first beheld "Edina's
palaces and towers," any one had whispered to me that I
should be the means of adding another to her many noble
edifices, I should have laughed the prophet to scorn—and so

would all of you had you been there. Do not, however, be
alarmed ; I am not going to pose before you in the rather dis-
credited character of the self-made man—(laughter)—with
dramatic effects of " I am that little boy " order. For I cannot
justly claim to be what is called in the usual grand phrase the
architect of my own fortune. Still, as a matter of fact, I was a
very little boy when I came to Edinburgh fifty-five years ago,
and instead of the proverbial sixpence which " the self-made
man " always has in his pocket, and which fructifies there in such
a wonderful manner, I had not a single brass farthing. I was
not only poor, but dependent, and it would be gross ingratitude
in me to the memory of him to whose bounty I mainly owe my
position in life if I were not to mention on this occasion, and
before this assemblage, the name of my grand-uncle, Mr John
Ritchie, one of the founders of the *Scotsman*, whom many of you
remember, and whose name I bear. I do not, however, mean to
disclaim all personal merit—that would be mock modesty again
—for I do not believe that any man gets on in the world without
some small amount of good qualities on his own part, whatever
they may be. (Laughter.) Yet I not the less readily and fully
acknowledge that I have been favoured by fortune. For one
thing, I have been most fortunate in my colleagues and asso-
ciates in business ; and I desire especially in this regard to
acknowledge my obligations to my friend and partner, Mr
James Law, to whose genius for organisation and manage-
ment the recent prosperity of the *Scotsman* is very largely due.
(Applause.)

Well, my Lord, when in course of time it became clear
to me that I could afford to do something personally towards
establishing a National Portrait Gallery, I had to consider how
the business could be managed, and it seemed to me that the
Honourable Board of Manufactures was, by its very constitution

and the cognate nature of its existing functions, the one body of all others through which such a project could best be carried out. At the same time, I desired to have some slight control over the disposal of the funds, and some small say in the arrangements, and I thought that the only way I could manage this was by getting myself appointed a member of the Board. And here I have to make a confession. To achieve that end I did what I believe no one connected with the *Scotsman* ever in the course of its whole existence did before or since. I asked a personal favour of the Government of the day—(laughter and applause) —and obtained a seat at the Board. The office of trustee is purely honorary—there is no salary attached; at this Board there is not the smallest chance of "pickings" of any kind whatever, and we therefore require no self-denying ordinance. As my motives, then, were not venal, but the reverse, you will, I trust, concede that my sin of solicitation was venial. Very soon after becoming a member, I confided my purpose to my valued friend, Sir William Fettes Douglas, and through him my original offer was made in 1882. You will thus see that I, like Jacob, worked seven years to obtain the desire of my heart, and also, like Jacob, I have had a Leah thrust upon me, and have had to provide house-room for two institutions instead of one. (Laughter and applause.) For several years Sir William was my sole confidant at the Board, but as he became anxious to have his responsibility shared by some other member, I ventured to communicate his wish and my secret to my right hon. friend the Lord President. To four persons only—except my wife, who, of course, does not count—has my confidence till to-day been limited. But it may be asked, Why did you make any secret of the business? That, my Lord, is a question which I do not think I am bound to answer, any more than to explain why the disclosure is made now. (Applause.)

It is quite out of my power, my Lord, to give my hearers any adequate notion of my obligations or my gratitude to Sir William Fettes Douglas and to the Lord President. The undertaking in all its stages and in all its difficulties—and these were much more numerous than any outsider could readily conceive—has from them received the most invaluable aid and service. My obligations to both are unbounded. The Lord President has at all times unweariedly lent it— as he freely and regularly does to the Board's business generally—the benefit of his great practical knowledge of affairs, his historical information, his legal learning and experience; and if we substitute the artistic for the legal element, the same remarks apply to Sir William Fettes Douglas. Both gentlemen have had a good deal of irksome correspondence with regard to this matter, which they have been very kind in undertaking. To Sir William also fell much of the trouble of the financial arrangements, which, with my friend Mr Law, he managed so well that it is only to-day that my own bankers will know where the money went to. I should also be sorry to omit my acknowledgments to our excellent secretary, Mr Inglis. The affair has added largely to his work and responsibilities; he has had to conduct many delicate and troublesome negotiations with the Lords of the Treasury, and with the Department over which you, my Lord Lothian, preside, and he has done all in the most carefully official, correct, and conservative fashion; the result being that the Board has not had to retrace a single step, and that we have gained every point for which we contended. (Applause.) Further, at the risk of my remarks taking somewhat of the aspect of a general thanksgiving, you will allow me to refer to my friend the architect, Mr Rowand Anderson. His work is before us; he, too, has had his troubles in carrying it out—some of them, no doubt, as is the fashion with architects, of

his own making—(laughter)—but not, perhaps, on that account
more easily borne or overcome.   Finally, to all my colleagues in
the Board, who attend its meetings and take an interest in its
affairs, I beg leave to tender my sincere thanks for the invariable
courtesy with which they have treated the views—troublesome
enough, perhaps—of the "anonymous donor," as expressed to
them generally through Sir William Fettes Douglas.   But for
the Board, but for its influence, and its sagacious conduct of the
whole business, this thing would probably never have been
done ; it certainly never could have been so well done.   To the
Board is really due the credit of having added this Gallery to our
national institutions ; it has perhaps the still more remarkable
credit of having, through the leverage supplied to it, extracted
from reluctant Governments no less than £15,000 towards its
establishment.   There never was a sum like this got for Scotland in this way before ; but that is no reason why the like
should not be done again.   (Applause.)   One word more, my
Lord Lothian, on a subject in which your Lordship, as President
of the Society of Antiquaries, has a special interest—namely, the
provision made within this building for the accommodation of
that Society and of the National Museum of Antiquities.   I
have the honour, like your Lordship, to be one of the office-
bearers of that body, and it was with the greatest pleasure that I
was able to do it service.   I remember how manfully and successfully your Lordship contended against the proposal at one
time made to shunt the Society and its collections to a pendicle
in the Museum of Science and Art ; and I do not doubt that
you will regard the association in this building of the Society of
Antiquaries with the National Portrait Gallery as a peculiarly
felicitous conjunction.   The two collections will be mutually
illustrative ; students of our national history will appreciate the
connection between the earlier and the later stages of civilisation

which they exhibit ; in the earlier the materials, and in the later
the men that have gone to the making of Scotland. In conclusion, I have again, my Lords and Gentlemen, to ask you to excuse
the, I fear, somewhat egotistical character of these remarks, and
all their other sins and shortcomings. I must ask you to take
into consideration the fact that I have had no previous experience of a like kind—never any similar task to perform. The
experience of your kindness—the sound of your applause—is
altogether new to me, and I trust that you will excuse the
awkwardness of a novice. (Loud applause.)

SIR JAMES KING, Lord Provost of Glasgow, was next called
upon by Lord Lothian. He said—I count it a privilege to
be here to-day to take part in a very interesting proceeding.
It is well for me that addresses so admirable and so interesting
have already been spoken, and that my task in saying a few
words will be a light one. But I feel that it is a compliment
to the city of which I have the honour of being the Chief
Magistrate that I should have an opportunity of assuring you
of the deep interest we take in the work which has this day,
I may say, been crowned with success, and that we gladly
congratulate the sister city—which we look upon, of course,
as the capital of Scotland—first, on having a citizen of whom
it may well be proud, with such large and liberal ideas, and
with the means of carrying them into effect, and not less in
possessing a body of trustees who have been so judicious in
the use of the funds which have been placed at their disposal.
There are certain respects in which we sometimes try to
emulate Edinburgh, and there are certain institutions which
might well be duplicated in Glasgow when the example has
been set here. There are other matters in regard to which we
have the advantage, perhaps, of holding the first place ; but, as
regards a collection of national portraits, there can be but one

collection, and in its formation every part of Scotland should count it a privilege to take part. I am sure there are, in many historical houses, valuable portraits of illustrious members of the family, of which there are more than one example, and one of these might fittingly be housed in such a building as this. And there are also many cases in which those who have been successful in life, and who possess artistic taste, have been able to procure portraits representing men who in former days have taken a prominent part in Scottish affairs, and they must in many cases feel that under no circumstances can they be so fitly shown or can they be so certain of preservation as in a national collection like the present. I hope that Glasgow and the West of Scotland will be able to bear their full share in presentations to the galleries which are this day opened. There is but one way, I think, that our gratitude can fittingly be shown to the generous donor—the donor of this munificent gift—and that is, by a general and combined effort to fill the house, now that it has been built. (Applause).

The SECRETARY FOR SCOTLAND then said—The duty now devolves upon me to declare this exhibition open. But before I do so, perhaps you will expect me to say a few words. It has been with the greatest possible pleasure that I have come down to-day—not in my personal capacity, of course, but at the request of Mr Findlay and the Board of Manufactures—that I should in my official capacity show the interest which the Government takes in the work we are here assembled to do— namely, the opening of this Gallery—because, as Scotsmen, we feel, and I think you all feel, that this is an occasion of no ordinary interest, not only to Edinburgh, but to Scotland. It is an occasion of interest to Edinburgh, because we have seen the result of the generosity of the anonymous donor, of whom I have now some difficulty in speaking, seeing that he is present.

Still, it is of great interest to Edinburgh, because it shows that in many other citizens there is still an increasing desire to beautify this beautiful town, and to spend what superfluous money they have made in a direction which would be of advantage to the city. But the interest goes much further than this. From what has been said by the Lord Justice-General and Mr Findlay himself, you will see that what has been desired by the erection of this building has not been to benefit Edinburgh only, but also to erect an institution which might be of advantage to the whole of Scotland. What has been said in the letters read by the Lord Justice-General of the opinions of Lord Hailes, Lord Buchan, Thomas Carlyle, and David Laing show that this desire is not a new one at all, but one which may be said to be ingrained in the character of our Scottish people. The interest, too, is not an interest in to-day; it is an interest in Scotland as it was, as it is, and as it is to be. For the first time in the history of our country we now have a home where we may place the portraits of those whose lives have made the history of our country. We have, or hope to have, life-like pictorial representations of those whose lives in all that is honourable have helped to make our little country as great as she is. The Lord Justice-General has alluded to the benefactor by whose generosity this building has been erected. I feel a difficulty in his presence in saying what I should like to have said. The Lord Justice-General had that advantage of me in what he said about him, because, although he knew he was here, he spoke to an audience who did not know. Still it would not be becoming in me, as representing you, and through you the people of Scotland, in accepting from him this magnificent gift, if I did not say how greatly we appreciate the generosity and forethought which has caused him to make it—(applause)—and I think not only

F

do we recognise the generosity, but we may also appreciate the wisdom with which that generosity has been attended. Mr Findlay himself has pointed out the direction in which that wisdom has gone, but I wish to say too that we fully appreciate it, because here, under this roof, we have not only a National Portrait Gallery, but we shall have very soon that magnificent collection of the antiquities of Scotland, which is to be housed in the other half of this building. That collection is, perhaps, the most complete and the best collection in the world of the pre-historic times of any nation in Europe. And, looking at that collection—which day by day is increasing in value—we may almost know what the lives were of our pre-historic ancestors in this country; and it is surely a fitting corollary to that collection that we should have in the other half of the building pictorial representations of those who have made, and are making, and will make in the future, the history of Scotland. The wisdom I speak of lies in this, that no greater incentive to patriotism can be found than in the instructed knowledge of what has gone before, and of the lives of those who have done what has conduced to the honour of the country. Therefore, ladies and gentlemen, does not what we have here and what we shall have in the other half make a most complete whole? Is there anything in this country, or in any other country, which can compare with the whole which will be given to us when we have gathered together materials of the past, present, and future history of this country under one roof? I think we may fairly congratulate the generous benefactor on what he has done in this respect for the city of Edinburgh and for Scotland. Ladies and gentlemen, you have not been upstairs yet to see the portraits which have already been collected. They have been very well selected, and the only fault I can find, so far, is that there are too few of them. I should like to take this

opportunity of expressing a hope—perhaps you will think it somewhat presumptuous in me to do so—that those who have now the charge of this National Portrait Gallery of Scotland will be exceedingly careful of the portraits they select. I should like to keep up a very high standard—a very high ideal—in this Gallery. I should like to guard against the temptation—which I am sure there will be at the first, because there are bare walls all around us, which we should like to see covered—of covering these walls by admitting portraits of those whose presence the opinion of subsequent generations might not justify. There is great difficulty, I know, in selecting portraits of people—especially of those who are still alive—to be placed on the walls. I should rather like—contrary, I believe, to the rules which exist in the portrait galleries in England—that, if possible, some portraits of living persons of our acquaintance should be placed on the walls. I know there are great difficulties attending it. I know the subject has been carefully considered often, and always, so far as I know, decided in the negative. But I should like to put before those who have charge of this institution the advantages there may be in the other direction. Many of those who have made the past history of Scotland have left no portraits behind them, and therefore there is no possibility of the public in the future knowing what they were like. There is another thing I should like to point out, and that is that the portraits selected to be hung upon the walls of such galleries are said, of course, to be portraits of such and such persons. But who can tell if they are like them—if they are an exact representation of those whom they pretend to be? Now, if a portrait was done in a man's lifetime, and placed on the walls during his lifetime, the public would be able to say whether it was a just and true representation of the person

or not. I do not agree with the words of Carlyle, which were read by the Lord Justice-General, that he would rather have an indifferent portrait than none at all. It seems to me that, if a portrait is to be of any value, it must show the mind as well as the face and the figure of the person represented. It is not a mere photograph you want. You want a portrait done by a great painter—a man who shall show what the mind behind the face was; because, as you all must know, very often the plainest face is the most beautiful in expression, in consequence of the mind behind it. I should dislike very much to see hung upon the walls of this Gallery portraits which were only a photographic representation. It is portraits which show the mind through the features that we really want. Perhaps you will forgive me for making these remarks, but I feel that, whatever may be the future of this Gallery, I should like to see it kept up to a high standard, and made a model of what a portrait gallery really ought to be. I have already said that a gallery such as this is, to my mind, the highest incentive to true patriotism we possibly can have. To look on the portraits of those who have done well by their country; of those who by any form of noble, true, and honest work have done good to their country; of those who by genius, in whatever way displayed —by military or literary genius; of those who by eminent goodness or piety, or patient self-denial, did good to their fellow-men; of those who never knew what defeat was—is in itself an elevating and stimulating influence. What we want is portraits of the men of whom Longfellow referred to as leaving "footprints on the sands of time":—

> " Footprints that perhaps another
> Sailing o'er life's solemn main,
> Some forlorn and shipwrecked brother,
> Seeing, may take heart again."

It is not only the "shipwrecked brother" who, looking, may take hope again; but the young life of the country may thereby grow in strength and truth and patriotism, and not only emulate, but excel in such virtues those who had gone before them, and may continue to make our dear old Scotland greater and greater. (Applause.) In the anticipation that these hopes may be fulfilled, and that year by year, as time goes on, we may see growing up many noble Scotsmen whose portraits may worthily adorn the walls, and with our most heartfelt thanks to the generous donor who has enabled us to have these anticipations and hopes, I beg now to declare the Scottish National Portrait Gallery to be open. (Loud cheers.)

LORD PROVOST BOYD said—I am sure you will agree with me that we are under a deep debt of gratitude to our noble Chairman for coming here to preside on the present occasion. The ordinary duties of his Lordship's office are numerous, anxious, and absorbing, and it is no ordinary addition to those duties that at this season of the year he should have consented to come from London, as he has done, to attend on this occasion when he must necessarily return again to his work by this night's mail. (Applause.) I am sure we are all deeply sensible of the obligation under which we lie to him for undertaking the important duty which he has discharged to-day, and I propose that we offer him our cordial thanks. (Loud applause.)

LORD LOTHIAN briefly acknowledged the vote.

The proceedings, which lasted about an hour and a half, then terminated, and the building was thrown open for inspection by the company. Many of those present took advantage of the opportunity of seeing the interior of the Galleries at the close of the opening ceremony.

The following is the text of the letter by Mr Findlay in 1882, which was communicated anonymously to the Board of Manufactures by Sir William Fettes Douglas, P.R.S.A. :—

"*7th December 1882.*

"DEAR SIR WILLIAM,—I address to you, as a member of the Board of Trustees for Manufactures, the present communication, because its subject is one in which you, as President of the Royal Scottish Academy, may be presumed to have a special interest.

"It has often been remarked of Scotland that no modern country of like limited area and population has produced so many men of far more than local eminence in literature, science, art, and arms ; yet Scotland has no National Portrait Gallery. It seems natural and fitting that the Board of Trustees, as custodians of the existing Gallery of Painting and Sculpture and as representatives of Government in such matters in Scotland, should take the initiative in any movement that may be made towards supplying this desideratum.

"Such an undertaking could not probably be adequately set on foot under something like £40,000 or £50,000. If the matter is taken up by the Board, I am ready to contribute £10,000 (say ten thousand pounds). With a like sum from the Board's own resources, other £10,000 might surely be raised by an appeal to the public, and with some £30,000 in hand the Board would certainly be amply justified in soliciting a considerable grant in aid from Government. This offer I must make anonymously through you as my guarantee. If the matter takes a practical shape in the hands of the Board within six months, I shall hand you the money for them.—I am, yours, &c."

INDEX OF PORTRAITS,

IN THE

SCOTTISH NATIONAL PORTRAIT GALLERY,

·REFERRED TO IN THIS PAMPHLET.

FINIS

www.ingramcontent.com/pod-product-compliance
Lightning Source LLC
Chambersburg PA
CBHW020557270326
41927CB00006B/881